Hélas Hellas Persephone

And Selected Poems

Laura Tattoo

3/12/2021

To dear Kelly,

Joy joy joy — that
is my beautiful sister
Kelly. So brilliant a
light, so profound a being.
I love you and
I am grateful,

Laura

Pannonica Press

Copyright © 2021 by Laura Tattoo

Published in the United States by Pannonica Press

All rights reserved.

www.pannonicapress.com

Printed in the United States of America   5 4 3 2

Library of Congress Cataloging-in-Publication Data

Tattoo, Laura,
Hélas Hellas Persephone And Selected Poems / Laura
Tattoo.—1st. ed.
p. cm.

ISBN   978-0-98000-14-5-7

First Edition

Cover art: "Kore Falling" by Jeanie Tomanek

Lost in Hell,—Persephone,
Take her head upon your knee
Say to her, "My dear, my dear,
It is not so dreadful here."

Edna St. Vincent Millay

For my mother who introduced me to
poems and for all survivors of chronic
illness and #MeToo.

Contents

HÉLAS HELLAS PERSEPHONE

Clotho to Atropos

Alone, alone
from the beginning
and even taken
alone
Coupled, alone
Returned, alone
Alone in the meadow
Alone in my cradle
Alone on my throne
My girlhood among girls
a momentary illusion
I was alone
at my birth
My busy mother
sister-wife to
my uncle-father
and I sparrow-eyed
a tiny girl
squalling yet
ignored
I was swallowed
whole from
that moment
and then again
when the earth
opened up and
a hectare of dirt
lilies, grasses
pigs and horses
whole trees and I
into the great maw

of Hades
alone, alone
did fall
endlessly
inevitably
utterly
alone

A cruel bargain

The eagle swoops
catching my hair
in its talons
bringing me to the feet
of my uncle again
lord of ghosts
I did not go willingly
the first time or ever
I was taken, snatched
from my girlhood games
laughing, running
diving into the dirt
covered with scratches
and bruised knees
our boyish lot
afraid of nothing
in love with life
and with each other
our coven of mothers
practicing their arts
busy busy busy
in their prim houses
brewing the potions
to keep our fathers
awake and asleep
paying no mind
to their prepubescent
daughters
striking bargains
to keep themselves alive
digging both

our graves
the eagle arriving
and with every rape
one more time
I die

Demeter's solution

After my capture
my mother took
her infinite grief
went to Eleusis
and built herself
a temple
She would have
all humans and
all gods
worship her
or starve
She became
self-absorbed and
struck down
in fear and rage even
her most ardent devotee
Do not cross Demeter
She will kill you
with a brick
even as she loved and
compromised me
in the same breath
I do not wish
to be worshipped
I leave that to her
I only want liberation
from Hades
from my mother's girdle
from the harvest and
primavera songs she taught
from the top to

the bottom of Olympus
from all these things
that bind and enslave me

Persephone on goddess worship

Do not worship me
Do not impale me upon
your marble altar
frozen in time
Do not bring me meat
butter or yogurt
sugary cakes or
exotic coffees
Do not dress me in
silken threads
that weave about my
wrists and ankles
Do not bring your
dying flowers
plucked from their stems
too soon
Do not play love songs
on your lyre to lull me to sleep
or beat the tapan
to enact a frenzied dance
Keep your candles
your lamps
your lebanon
your cedar bark
your peaches
your apples
your peacock feathers
your horsetail fans
your water baths
your milk baths
your vows of abstinence

your virgin sacrifices
Just, I tell you again
do not worship me
do not set me up
do not fetishize me
do not ignore me

"A Girl's Guide to Heaven and Hell"

One Hades after another
in yet another guise
new doorways of Hell
Go east west north south
It is infinite degrees of hellevity helgevity
And that main gate Hellas
at the top of Mount Olympus?
Make no mistake:
you have not entered Paradise
There is no way of liberation here
no summit of compassion
There is only Zeus in disguise again
prognosticator
prevaricator
filthy liar
your worst nightmare

Dans le jardin

Toujours ces clés d'antiquité
Les pleurs viennent
on ne peut pas les empêcher
Les reines fières
souriantes en masques d'albâtre
leurs robes longues, les cheveux serrés
Mais leurs filles sont nues
chassées, emportées, violées
par les dieux et les fils de dieux
en formes d'animaux

More Hélas Hellas

I

Sky or water
it doesn't much matter
I was falling I was flying
with a stone around my neck
drowning in illness
We could say you reached down
and pulled me out
It wouldn't be an overstatement
You were not Calypso
and I was not Odysseus
though when I consider
everything we lived through
the analogy is fitting
I rested with you
on that volcanic island
erupting in the middle of Europa
and I was grateful
As the sweet centenarian habits
of high fat, early sleep and sex
became a fascist doctrine
I found myself floundering again
feeling controlled and angry
in the face of your volcano project
I was no longer buying it
and my mind wandered home
to the doorsteps of my children
because those deep umbral cords
and the lyric flow of breast milk
keep us united in an eternal song

Even if I could see into the future
as you would later bless
and curse me with
the rejection complete and total
of sons for their mother
I still longed to return
And every morning
I ran through the streets of Lamia
heart beating madly
with fire and sweat
and nothing could help me
not warm Greek bread
not antique beauty
Sweet Calypso
I had to leave
mais j'ai fait un beau voyage
and even if you are correct that
the earth is rapidly cooling
as we pass through
galactic cloud matter
and the increased celestial electricity
is raising the magma flows
in their underwater chambers
sparking discontent
among the nations
I would rather die
than never write poetry
again by lamplight
and I will die
that is what you
do not understand, being a god
I am a woman
tied to Ithaca
and I am mortal

I know I promised
to marry you, Apollo
but I did not foresee
how punishing you would become
when I broke my pledge
leaving you to languish
on a smoldering Olympus
in the volcanic winter
of your snowball heart
I was a lovestruck silly girl
who thought she could see
into the future and you said
"Go ahead, Cassandra
I have a road map"
I looked and looked
but I didn't see it
or maybe I looked
and I couldn't do it
or maybe I saw how
cold Greece would become
in the immediate future
and democrat and Jew that I am
I couldn't handle your antisemitism
your hatred of all Muslims
and even those "barbaric" Christians
though you still pretend to be Orthodox
If anything Greece was lost
to those black-cloaked priests
who are paid by the state
and thus subjugate and are subjugated
Strange country:

You blame the Ottomans
and I don't blame you a whit
but someday you have to get over it
or start making your own clothing
Everywhere everywhere
the labels scream
"Made in Turkey"
"Made in Germany"
Let the wealthy of Greece
rise up and invest
in their countrymen!
Throw off the bureaucratic
shackles of church and state!
Don't believe me?
Well there's the rub
for me to see the horrors
and no one to believe what I tell them
just as I didn't believe you
your narrow road
your climate litanies
or your love
It's fast karma or some such
religious nonsense
more blasphemy
more cannibalism
more 21st-century anarchy
We both see the frozen future
but no one can hear us

I was a tree
frozen in bark
neglected, celibate
roots of sadness so deep
the sky's tears
could not reach them
Apollo chased and ravaged me
and I became a woman
named Daphne
I blossomed with
sea pine in the fall
orange blossom in the spring
swooning under my
own salted perfume
I climbed hills
I sought beauty
I read until my eyes
grew red and bleary
Every cell *vivant*
my skin bronzed
my heart charged
with a lightning rod
For a brief moment
it made me young
and the world became turquoise
water, light and sulphur
burnt fields
paradisiacal mountains
endless groves of olive
and the language that entered
my ears was music

and I tried hard to learn it
but it was never enough
Oh make me a tree again
Oh make me a statue
now that Apollo has gone
and taken with him
his songs of love
Life is complicated
and then it is not
and then it breaks apart
into a new composite

Sapphic verses

I can/ hardly/ speak again/ far from/ dreaming
Eros/ sang me/ songs by heart/ dozens/ laughing
I am/ not a/ fool for naught/ I fell/ I flew
Far from home/ and hearth

To Hel/las a/nother life/ aching/ beckoned
You who/ healed my/ body and/ soul long/
anguished
Drew me/ with your/ siren's song/ comic/ vision
Promised me life/ and breath

Ever/ forward/ limbs unfurling/ dead then/
living
Flowers/ opened/ petals fell/ perfume/ spreading
Lilac/ laurel/ jasmine bright/ rose and/ sea pine
Blind and then/ seeing

Even/ if the/ ruinous/ dust could/ pardon
I would/ only/ have the day/ and then/ no more
Silent/ birds drift/ by their hope/ into/ madness
Seeking love/ airborne

Timeless/ we have/ fallen in/ time's en/trapment
Lips to/ hands u/nite us once/ and not/ again
First em/braces/ leave us new/ after/ morning
Then mourning/ takes us

Sparrow in Hell

I know nothing about
foundations or cellars
I'm not squirreling away
nuts for winter
or laying slabs of concrete
And that storm that's overhead?
Let it bring the best and
brightest lightning
Let it burn this shack to ashes
or shake it from its berth
beneath the dirt
Let it bleed spirit from
black and blue space
Let hell unleash its nine circles
and let Cerberus bark and yelp to
keep me back from the river Styx
My foot is already passing over it
and damn it, as always
as cruel and as fast as disaster
I cannot attach
and I am not afraid

Lament

*For the Lamed-waf are the hearts of the world
multiplied, and into them, as into one
receptacle, pour all our griefs.*
--Le dernier des justes, André Schwarz-Bart

I am *Lamed-vov*
the last of the just
and I'll tear my hair out
before I'm done
if God will permit me
and of this indeed
nothing is less certain
for I must stand
and bear it all
as recompense for
what I've done and
what came before
when I was nary a thought
a dove on an olive branch
that traversed the great
Mediterranean cradle
and its salt-encrusted air
clung to my skin
and made it brittle

The ultimate rejection
by everyone I loved
is not a simple fruit
to carry in one's womb
but a heavy pit
of infinite sadness
every bit as unbearable

as Demeter's grief
or any mother who
lost her child to death
or misfortune
or rejection
choose your poison
or an unjust God will
choose it for you
and then you will
cleave to him because
he is all you have left
abandoned in the middle
of the great forest

Your little clay hut
molded by your hands
out of water and mud
a tepid oil lamp burning
on the hearthstone
beads running through
your fingers upon which
you count the names of
everyone you've loved
the dearly departed
the vagabonds
and the children
alive and buried
and each one a blessing

A different species

It is not my fault
I was born a fruit bat
among a family of
vampire bats

Zeus suckled by a goat
never received her sweetness
only insatiable lust
and drunken vengeance

Hera once queen of heaven
now chained to a mountain
she became alpha femme
and hausfrau

She threw her son Hephaestus
down to his death
then raised him back up
when she discovered his gifts

Demeter my mother
roamed the earth in pain
then settled for the threshing
floor—it wasn't worth it

Poseidon, leave her alone!
Hades, leave me alone!
You can't make a vampire
out of a fruit bat!

I'm starving myself

to get out of this hellhole
I'm starving myself
to regain control

But the truth is
I'm starving
I can no longer resist
the seeds of the pomegranate

Persephone refuses the return

Let the earth starve
if it must
I am not responsible
I've lost enough
life in its mouth

My childhood
my maidenhood
my motherhood
even my death
resurrected year after year
like a puppet on a stick

I didn't deserve it
I didn't ask for it
I never saw it coming
and all the people
women and men
and all the nation states
and all the gods my family
should repent
and wake up

These rituals
you teach our
maiden youth
that mimic my abduction
and return
the great drama played out
with dancing and flowers
animal and child sacrifices

they must be stopped

Let the wheat be stunted
Let the sun burn out
Let the volcanoes flow red hot
I am not going back

My name is Persephone
Kore, Despoina
Say my name out loud
I will not damn you
I am no longer
willing to damn you

You are free
and I am free
from sacred rites
from abduction
and rape
from the underworld
and Olympian prisons

There is just the earth
turning in all its seasons
and you and I free
to turn with it
and every day
the rose-gold Dawn
carried on the backs
of the Four Winds

TWELVE POEMS
OF MALADY AND DESPAIR

1 Almost Driving

I took an old highway tonight
through evergreen and scotch broom,
one of those quaint coastal roads
that weave in and out of little
towns like Mist and Vernonia.

I drove to escape my boredom,
and though it never worked before,
escape is a heavy metal in my blood,
fueled by the boxes of guilt
I piled inside the trunk,
enough to last the winter
if I could keep myself driving.

In Florida the back roads
smell of oranges and jasmine;
in Oregon it's Douglas fir and rain.
The sliver of moon didn't light the sky
but it was a sign nonetheless
until it rotated behind me;
other signs were rusting in the damp
as I snaked my way past them.

I took my music player
from its soft denim sack
and played the song list I'd made
the day before I left:
all the sad ballads,
for I knew they would sing about the pain
that I dared not verbalize,
swallowing two pills against its swell:

they made me work
the gas pedal and brake.

I was driving toward a new life,
a little hideaway
on the side of a cliff
where each day I could decide
whether to jump or to live,
where a lamp might be lit
and words added to it:
but my little drive was never
about writing poems.

No there would be no little house,
no perfect moon,
no ocean lookout,
no final requests for
whale crossings or bouillabaisse:
only split-second decisions.

It was about turning stoically around
and finding my way home,
unloading the guilt boxes (again),
turning on the television
and awaiting a conventional death.

Like so many ghost dolls
I once knew how to drive,
I was going places until
malady came and stole away my life,
left me in angst and in pain,
but like a cruel joke
left the car in the driveway.

2 Fishing

I tell my doctor I'm in pain
and she tells me to see
a psychiatrist

The room is 7 x 7 x 10
there's a door but I
can't open it

Somewhere there's a net
being tied together
to catch a fish

And a marathon
will take place at dawn
but there will be no runners

My body is tired of
living out this rat race
of pain

It wants to swim
out to sea and sink
but it won't make it

Somewhere the crickets
have begun to flood
the night with sound

Somewhere a dogwood
is covered with a parasite
and doesn't bloom

A dog barks
a door opens
a fish is caught

I'm sitting here
without hope because
hope left long ago

Shall I eat a pizza
listen to some jazz
fish for poems

Shall I say thank you
for what was once
a meaningful life

Pain takes everyday issue
with modest undertakings
like bathing or breathing

Pain takes away the
last ounce of goodwill
you have for yourself

A lawn mower starts
and gets louder and
softer across the street

The sun is shining and
everybody's up and at 'em
with joy and thanksgiving

I tell my doctor I'm in pain

and she tells me to see
a psychiatrist

The room is 7 x 7 x 10
there's a door but I
can't open it

3 Toxic Mantras

"Somatoform disorder"
the very words chill the heart
like an abusive priest crying
"Suffer the little children
to come unto me"
a mantra so painful
even your flaming body
grows hotter
flushes with ice
and boiling water
lifts you from the chair
you've been captive in
for twenty years
as you throw yourself
at the marauder
at the bankrupt siren who's
singing to Solomon
and nothing can stop
the rage you feel
as you tumble to the floor
flailing your aching arms
standing on useless knees
and weeping icicles
sharp and hard
from years of slaughter
at the hands of doctors
wagging their tongues
of disbelief
proffering toxic mantras
into waiting mouths
into dimpled brain cells

as adrenal glands contract
and the natural matter
of surety and survival
is stolen from you

4 Med Time

I wake up from that
last dream I can't remember
and the TV is still on
I want it to be five hours
but it is only three
and my eyes and neck
are aching
Did I take my 4 am meds
or did I forget?
My body says forgotten
but the med box is empty

Then I remember my husband
holding out his hand
like a bronzed buddha
until I was awake enough
to sit up and swallow
I've seen him sit there
for an hour until
his patience is spent
and he says
"Honey, I'm tired!"
I always feel like a lump then
and apologize

So the pills are swallowed
and the TV is still on
but it isn't time
for "Democracy Now"
and it isn't even time
for "Washington Journal"

It's hours hours hours
until a timer sounds
the half-life ends
and I turn off the TV
and start it all again:
the insidious waiting
for the end of pain

5 Psychobabylon

"How are you even alive today?" she asked,
eyes bulging from her head,
body taut with dread and excitement.
I answered, "Because I write,
because I get to express myself while
looking for truth and justice."

(On the great American way, hey-hey,
the flat-beat drum across the plain,
the White Buffalo and the Wannabe...)

I'd come to see her because I needed help
getting off my pain meds, I wanted to
detox from a drug that had made me
even worse, hopeless and miserable,
with vertigo so deep I couldn't see straight,
rapid heart beat and blood pressure so low
the nurses always exclaimed, "Great!"
as they ripped the cuff off my arm.

(Maybe if I were an athlete in red Nike shorts,
doing warm-ups and five-mile days, but not
the pathetic gray lump sitting on this chair...)

I recounted for the new counselor
all the facts of my sad history,
the rapes, the violence, the mental illness,
the times I was hospitalized or homeless,
the frightened child, the abandoned infant.
She needed it all to assess what kind of
judgment I had in my debilitated state.

(And why I spilled the beans in that
holy church, God only knows; I guess
memories get triggered easily in my world...)

I was triggered tonight by Spike Lee,
five years after Katrina: watching again how
the government turned their backs on the
black and poor, tore down their homes,
closed their hospitals, left the mentally ill
adrift on the Gulf without a shithole or paddle,
shipped the rest off to Houston or Nevada.

(Left it to Sean Penn to drag the bodies out
and to Brad Pitt to rebuild the entire Ninth Ward,
and fuck the Army Corps of Engineers...)

I've been living like a corpse on the water:
For 14 years I've been stuck on a couch,
too sick and depressed to fend for myself,
driving up credit cards to afford bogus cures
because my government wouldn't invest enough
to find out if this was an AIDS-like retrovirus
as anyone who lived with it suspected it was.

("There's nothing wrong with your
autonomic nervous system!" "Thanks to oxycontin
you'll live in a box." "Don't sweat the small stuff!")

My doctors turned their heads,
turned them over to the head experts
because they didn't know what to look for,
not that the geniuses at Disease Control
had given them a handbook, but rather
told them we were neurotic and tired

and finally, furiously, they blamed us for it all.

(Isn't that what callous authority does
when it doesn't have the know-how?
It blames the victim...)

After that, you just stay home, you resist calling.
No matter how sick you get, you get through it.
You think, they've got nothing to offer me;
this is as good as it gets.
I may be housebound but I've got my films,
my music, my poems. I've got a kind husband who
brings me tea and kisses me on the forehead.

(Like an animal that gets sick, you want
to crawl away in the dark, but like a human being
you never forget your former life...)

Tonight I'm sailing down the Mississippi
on an old life raft patched with band-aids.
I'm still taking the pain meds. They want
me to see a psychiatrist next, assess the old
labels and chemical imbalances.
What I need is a miracle, a friend, and a
reasonably good doctor who believes me.

(Or I'll die like everybody else,
I'll go the way of old CFS-ers: a heart attack
or a gun and an old Indian song.)

We brown ones, we broken ones,
we Congolese girls, we Tanzanian fishermen,
we victims, we predators,
we addicted, we atheists,

we hungry, we homeless,
we gamblers, we murderers
we invalids, we children.

(Survival of the fittest in a
savage landscape, just so much water
in the common well...)

6 Dirge

There's been enough gold
for one lifetime
and enough blood too
Poverty shall haunt me
bending her long diatribes
into the hollows of my ears
like the ghost of a wind
launching the moon
into a cold pale gloaming

The cupboard is empty
and deep inside a
gnawing beetle is cutting
through my room
bringing down the house
onto the dirt cellar
with its smell of cider
and formaldehyde
and bitter mushrooms

I do not want the spring
to come upon this land
I want a dirge for everyone
who has died here
who spent his finger flesh
in orchard and field
who buried her children
burnt her furniture
and fed cornmeal to chickens

Poverty my long lost

grandmother
take me down where
the workhorse grazes
I want to lie on the hay
and remember it all
I want to eat potatoes
and fall asleep under
soundless stars

Nothing can hold me
hearty and hale
when everyone I loved
has left this place
Only poverty shall have me now
my shirt sullied and rent
with dirt on my face and
worms and beetles
my fair-weather friends

And in my hands
a silver spoon
the last one in the drawer
to dig a pit
that's five by two
to better fit a
blind man's daughter
who dwelt with him
fifty years or more

Now she lies in the earth
and sheds no tears
nor listens for the push
of the starting buds
It's over and done

she has had enough
the whistling teakettles
and the lily bells that grow
between the corn rows

7 The Proverbial Undoing

This barn needs cleaning out
from cunt to cranium
a vascular sweep
vacuum out the viral load
the glut of sweet feces
all the dreams all the belief
leave it empty
and unblemished
the clogged arteries
the toxidromic stomach
replace all the earth
with fresh dirt

Then plant no seed there
just leave it alone as
a sign in the wilderness
bring no vase of flowers
to place in the corner
nor enshrine the undoing
with public symbols
no fat buddha no crucifix
do not write a hymn
or proverb or allegory
on no mountain sing that
she died for your sins

Best forgotten or vague
the history of the undoing
children will grow afraid
and dogs howl at nothing
the cult of the fatal must
at all costs be prohibited

8 The Limits of Hope

There's something about watching your teeth fall out
one by one, fragment and break off,
that's pretty damned depressing...
All the sharp edges come into view of the tongue,
that all-seeing organ like a great antenna,
bending into the crevices of your broken beauty.
Perhaps I am committing a great sin in
growing old and toothless when
I should be able to give up illusion and march
forward into the light of pure being,
the way Gandhi did or Mary Baker Eddy;
or else, as they did too, swallow the morphine
when the pain became too great to bear:
for even great souls are not immune to weakness
once pain sets in to stay and that
great hopelessness is upon you,
with the realization that it is hope itself that kills
and keeps you striving for ever greater control
over your health and welfare and other people.
Better to give up the hopeless quest and know
that everything ages, becomes diseased and dies
and no amount of spiritual angst or enlightenment
is going to stop it.

9 Illumination

Just once I'd like to see
the sun at 3 am
break through my window
light up my sallow face
grace me with music
unlike the fickle moon
with its dysrhythmic phases
but a hot glaring sun
burning up the paper
under my aerial fingers

Jasmine blooms through the night
I can still smell its perfume
flooding through the car window
as I drove from Florida to California
I never made it: I was stranded
in a Texas panhandle
shivering in a pup tent
and when I woke up in the middle
of that barren frozen universe
I turned around and headed home

Memories may linger
but our best laid plans
turn to ashes on earth
Poets are made from this
deep dark tenebrous
anxious for illumination
whether in rhyme or reasoning
but it is the loss of hope
that heaviest of burdens

that oft unveils it to them

Thrice have I seen the Seine
wend through the city of Paris
For three months I roamed
midnight alleys and quays
penning poems to goddesses
I spoke in a tongue that brought
vagabonds running
I was drunk with love
but what is sad to me today
is that I could not sustain it

10 Necessary Boundaries

My little closet is being invaded
by beautiful alien youths in dreadlocks
I wish I could open the windows
and sing hallelujah with the angels
but I have nothing to say when
my sickness is so thick, lodged in
a slow, one-track brain, throat raw
and closed, body in full pain

I tuck away the poems and
big screen TVs, brush my hair
paint on a Mona Lisa smile
but my eyes cannot hide my
fear of the intrusion upon
this stark and naked place

My guilt is over the top
for I love youth so much
who reach out from busy lives
to visit a cripple in her sickroom
I wish my mind were an open sky
free of these harsh boundaries

The closed quarters of this
caged bird will go down in
history as a complex loom
on which I wove the terms of
my own shame and loneliness

In the end I always relent and say
let it not be so, throw open

the gates and let them come
and come what may because
I judge myself the worst in
proportion to this suffering

Yet I cannot draw the blinds on pain
emanating from my half-closed
eyes and vacuous speech
the most basic of truths is
I am sick with a virulent virus
and today like most days
I have no good thing to say

Dear youth, please forgive me
when I sink in that blue pool
the wallows of self-pity
that turn from liquid to ice
any trace of self-worth

I want more than anything
to dance a waltz with you
and rejoice in your successes
speak French like a Frenchman
but no matter the desire
I'm mute and sick and fed up
and I cannot receive you today

11 Off the Straight and Narrow

I need to take a long vacation
from this bodily angst
sit on top of a hill and meditate
like in the old days without
thoughts about hunger or thirst
or what time it is
or what pills to take
or what I did then
or what was done to me

I want to feel wind and rain
on naked vulnerability
to sit absorbed
in a single tangible thing
my breath in and out
not the worn-out dreams
surrendered in illness
nor where I should go
or how I should get there
but here in this moment
which is the only place I own
yet over which I have no control
nor would I want it because
therein lies my freedom

There's a path I can take
that was custom made for me
the trees and shrubs cut out
by wind and desiccation
sand crushed from grand caverns
sifted and gathered and

making this way meandering
yet I have no fear of losing my way
because the sun rises in the east
and sets in the west
as does Venus with her fierce love lamp
and these things do not vacillate

I put one foot in front of the other
to climb the scraggy path
up to the summit of the dune
with a symphony of waves
and seagulls gliding in air currents
and hundreds of sanderlings
running frenetically through foam
and when I sit like that
brought there by my own two feet
I feel a sense of ionizing peace
as one of a gazillion stars in a
heavenly vista that rolls on and on
eternally evolving
creating path after path
reaching one or another resting point
for weary pilgrims

12 Malady and Despair

The sun has come back
from its holiday
It is shining on
the glory tree
outside my window
greening its leaves
with photorays
more life for the
indefatigable world

I rest pathetically in
my dark room
my faded curtains
let in a bit of light
my tired eyes
my faulty wiring
the rum-rum
beneath my skin
disfigures everything

Yet there is no one
to see and thus
my rupture in the light
my volte-face
never takes place
I'm like a little child
too shy for the world
who keeps safe in spite
of her loneliness

Soon it will be dark
and the cold air
will enter the
veins of the house
My fever will turn
to ice and chill
There are socks and scarves
and an old gray sweater
at the end of my bed

I will put them on
and lay down
perchance to dream that
there is love
the hero's quest
as it was
before the blitzkrieg
before illness came
and took everything

I am too tired to
continue to write
The light is now
muted late afternoon
The only sounds I hear
are the churning fans
and a few cars
on the highway
going home

I'll say goodnight
before you go
I'm still polite in the
face of my demise

I've put my light face on
with a few lines
I've shown I am still
alive even though
there is no desire

Goodnight, goodnight
I feel no sorrow
in saying it
Tomorrow we begin again
to follow the sun
from east to west
floating from light to shadow
and seeking transcendence
over malady and despair

ONE TOO MANY MUSES

.

The Last Ashram

We've broken away from the swami games,
the clashing of kartals, the clanging of
tongues,
jealous retribution in a kitchen
until one feels
not a whit oneself,
fit or be fitted,
incline or die.

We can leave our shoes outside but
we bring the baggage in,
and to win, what a prize!
To sit beside a laughing man,
a place right next to the plastic man,
a man guaranteed to make you cry
in your sleep, in your dreams.

"Come, oh ye sheep,
to the butcher block
of heavenly peace."

That Voice

O to forget
To leave and to forget
I'm inclined to the right
Your voice is the voice
of intrinsic manipulation
It tells me
never to forget
the winding side-saddle days
the days when I loved you
with leisure
and put all my trust
in an unending love
I'm not the one
who stole those days away
and made me pay
for some fantasy crime
for which I've never been forgiven
by you or me
What did I do, do, do
that left me lonely and
broken on an opposing shore
without you, nothing!
And still you insist
with that voice of certainty
that you know me better
than I know myself
—That I was too wild
—That I had to be broken
—That you were always the one
to do it
Six years ago you left me

with life throbbing in my hands
two frail sons and a shattered heart
We both know it was a lie
Was always a lie
But still you insist
and still I incline
but now I resist
that voice every time

The Alibi

Jump for joy into the frying pan
Charge like lightning to the rod
Break and cry for dreams washed by
Terrible truth your alibi

Your alibi for what you do
You grow like thunder on the plain
The crisis comes and you can cry
Terrible truth your alibi

Ride the tram across the town
And take a step and then fall down
Waves will break and tears will dry
Terrible truth your alibi

You'd like to stand upon a wall
And yell to the night that tears must fall
But quiet weeping do you ply
Terrible truth your alibi

How much the grass in spring does grow
It fills the plains and obscures walls
But summer comes and grass will dry
Terrible truth your alibi

Too many fucking needs

Need need nothing but a fucking need
Where there's one there's another
Don't doubt it/ Need shouts louder
Ignore it, floor it, stomp it home free
Just take away the need
and let me be

Were there a dark cloud
I could number it away
But need shines brighter
than a summer's day

I'm overdressed, I break
the threads/ Shatter the future
Need, need, something outside
to set me free

Call me neurotic, it doesn't much matter
for need is here to stay
I'm just another runaway/ Just a little
kid again, full of need

On the Train

Dramamine or die!
Endless day and trains to ride
Solipsistic mothers
ride their children to the
end of the line
My stomach tightens and turns
My eyes burn into this young girl

I found her eyes
and hers found mine
Frames of sadness, a glance of shame
A minute's time, a beat away
she smiled and lit my day
How can I say?
We survived

Rose Song

Tradition bungles on for rose queens
Boats roll wide, bridges tumble in
Time will end in a breath
Hold the traffic 'til you drop with death
Across the river of bliss

Bilkovitch on Salmon Days

Bilkovitch, I knew him well
Just a little clown from Lower East Bay
He took himself out of town
each year on Salmon Days
to escape the humdroning
of a mediocre parade
paradisiacal façades
and the red-haired girl who
flagged his heart
with her knotted scarf

All the talk about Salmon Days
found him reeling on the sand
He crouched, picked up a shell
and glistening in his rage
commenced a tirade against pretty
girls who play songs
that go all wrong
Promises the gods never make
except when the wind blows east
on Salmon Days

I knew him as a fool then
with his wisecracking mouth
flubbing like jelly in the East Bay wind
He tried to hang himself once, twice
three times over Salmon Days
Each beat of his heart
built a shelf that held a rock
stamped with his obscurity
Transfixed, his thoughts washed away

with each throw of the rune

He's mad, Mr. Bilkovitch
A chronic loner with only one glitch
The needs won't let him be
The sea has bled him free
to merge with the elements
and to author a tale
of the red-haired girl who refused
to look him in the eye
And who died in a wasteland
East Bayers call Salmon Days

Tears

Tears would roll rancid if I let them,
They're so old they've grown mold—
Battery acid can't burn deeper
than the lagoon in my soul—
The mind accepts its stale symbols,
The world comes dripping in—
It's a sin to swim where that water is—
Let it roll to clarity instead.

The Crow in the Bay

For Lucie Brock-Broido

Waif comedienne
Bankrupt siren
off the seawall she crows

Chanties of chronic distaste
Butchery
and banal belief

Slip beneath her wing
And worship in common with
aquatic beasts of burden

Bella linda loma foma
Roll like sea trash
your languid diatribes

I will love you forever
And your dirty songs will be
my wit's end

My Muse

Everyone says the train's my muse
but the squeal of the wheel
obscures her real voice
That nag, nag, nagging every day!
I've known her better as Routine—
Her whip is unrelenting
so I just give in
Resist and it's a joke
You might as well
hang yourself
with a garland of clover

The Ghost In The Wreck

This room's got crow's eyes
big and wide
a frenetic smile
that's suicide
walls that mock
and floors that roll
above the briny sea

I remember when
he carried me in
and promised me sin
and promised me bliss
The sky drew dark
the wind had teeth
above the briny sea

Alone in such
a tyrant's bed
I called myself
his biggest fan
but cursed the day
he set his plan
above the briny sea

He must have thought
the gods would watch
as he pursued
his pleasure course
The sounds of land
escaped the man
above the briny sea

Our room was pierced
upon a rock
and crows did eat
my battered corpse
An empty place
that time's forgot
above the briny sea

The Long Night

Tantamount to nothing
this train rides
back and forth forever
in a long dark jacket
The future is tunneling
through the mountain
with a vengeance
Death is burgeoning and
blasting with a pressure
that's unrelenting
Everything will be declared
We can hide no more
from the shrill hard whistle
in the night
Our dreams will break
Our sleep will be nil

Voice of the Damned Cliché

You've got to be prolific
to even hint at the truth
Verses of finite wonder
aren't enough

Give your voice gladly
your pride and your fall
Reveal a little madness
in the afterglow

Just learn goddammit!
It's not enough to
sit idly by and
pretend it's for rent

It's going bye-bye fast
Life is running out
of lady luck
You're next someday you know

Harvest Moon

I saw the moon rise
as I crossed that bend
where the road runs straight
into a dusky sky

I swear it was
the harvest moon
as huge as our
round globe!

Triumph and revelry
it dwells in our gravity
melding the near
and the far

Normally we're a shadow
bent elbow
to the universe

The Poet's PTSD

Damn these rhymes
in a damned fermented mind—
Rolls of sea trash
caught on fishing lines—
I sift and peck
like a frantic hen
for a living, breathing catch,
a bit of bloodletting,
a stab at forgetting,
or a birthing song
for a dead poet:
There's my dead fourteen
who through it all—
the vagrancy, the stinging bee,
the cold, hard street, the sex for free—
wrote to live,
and lived to catch
her own poetic license,
a little noble insight
on that damned resting bed
where she could burn to ashes
every scoundrel she met,
yet emerge to invent,
three-lived, tripling in glee,
poems for an unrelenting bent
and the three reptilian men
who caught her eye
in an all-night diner
and saw her need for sleep:
Thanks to them
she's the wreck of the west,

thanks to them
she's transcended sex,
thanks to them
she's dead, yes!

But the poems, goddammit,
the living, breathing poems,
the lines of sea trash,
the noble insight,
the poetic license,
fuck it, take it, it's all for free!
I never held anything back
but this fermented anger
that finished me.

The Making of Rain

For Akira Kurosawa

I was an inmate of sadness
But I dried all my tears
And put away the madness
Of those melancholic years

The locked doors and the voices
The old crown of perdition
The cold reason of choices
The treason of tradition

And I blew it to an atom
With one puff of my mouth
And left behind my Sodom
For the garden of the south

Now I rest in this bright place
Perfumed with gardenia
Birds on my window lace
Sonatinas de España

And I realize the sadness
Is a part of the framework
And the isolating madness
Is a bulwark of a birthmark

And I justify the dullness
With the sadness that I've lost
Like an amnesiacal witness
To the holocaust of frost

I know that I could leave there
With one wave of my hand
And blow the frost to seafare
At the edge of this bright land

But I covet it like butter
On a renunciant's bread
And close up every shutter
And put myself to bed

To dream of the northland
And the cold bitter snows
That reduce every man's plan
And cover mouth and nose

To rest on her bosom
To hear her heart ticking
Puts an end to the flotsam
Puts an end to the thinking

I lay in this garden
And give myself to pain
And watch the south sky darken
And lend itself to rain

One Too Many Muses

One too many muses
I've got two
One who's kinda bluesy
One who's stuck on you

One who's shy and lonely
One who bought new shoes
She's so thin and bony
The other one can't lose!

One who rails cacophonous
and sets her toe on line
One who rises with the sun
and loves the spring's bright light

One who takes you to a cliff
and drops you off the edge
and so does visit bitter blight
on our new age sagesse

One who dreams of weekend bliss
and mornings spent in bed
with late late nights and dal with rice
that spicy taste of sin!

One who calls and one who comes
Expectation/mirrored awe
Riveted/spirited, psychopath/limited
God... and human after all

She hands me the punchline

like so much melted butter
I give her a smiley face
and lift her from the gutter

"It's another dark day..."
"But the sun is shining!"
"It's another ace of spades..."
"But goddammit you won!"

Of Mind

Fantasy, it's all fantasy
We live our lives as we dream
make our decisions
strum the strings of mind
plunge blind into the misbegotten
jump for joy in the sublime

I've long ago forgotten
to believe in fate and reason
We pursue our fantasy
like fruit in season
The test of time rests unrelenting
upon the tree of life

Believe and you will see
Project and you will be
Mind above all, fate below
Secure yourself in the afterglow
The senses fade, the will begins
Thought is our begin again

MORTAL AND IMMORTAL POEMS

Beneath The Surface

I was a fisher's wife
and I know fish stories better than anyone,
better perhaps than He who scattered them,
for I have recited them as
verbs to a language:

Diving until my belly
runs through the weeds,
slides across mud,
taut with a slow exhalation, then easy pump,
and a searching with the hands.

As my lungs grow thick,
I rise to the light,
a bubble to the mass,
one wave of the arms and
I'm gone:

> *Here behind you!*
> *Across the pond!*

I view the rain in a mirrored hand
beneath the clear black surface,
where each drop forms a perfect arc
and the world becomes
an open mouth.

Visit from the Bard

I'm releasing pathos with
every bead of sweat, every
cigarette I smoke, all the
moments of my life building into
this paradigm of parody

I charge with the elements
die with the seasons, I'm high
on sleep deprivation and black tea
so that I see past reason
into the Bard's own raging vision

Yes I'm changing with fits and starts
and here he is, fit for kingdom come
He too is drenched with sweat
injecting pink-white pollen from a
violet syringe into a primordial vein

then takes another stiff drink
of ink, breathing into the
moonlight as it stretches
into a cloud bank, the ebony
night lit up with shooting stars

He spots Venus buzzing by
then Saturn and Mars
He does not count on stars
but does a nosedive onto newsprint
scribbling his name again and again

wondering if the morning light

will find him drunk on absinthe
and whether or not Pandora's box
still sits atop his nightstand
and if he will open her up

I am the first to fly out
I am the mother sun in the
dawning, the ghost at 6am
I am the butter on his toast
a slave to his feathered head

but never enough of his words
I feed him honey on a spoon
so he will feed my wit
transform my sweat to pearls
and my smoke to poems

and I pass into his trance
embrace his dogged footsteps
trample on his lavender lips
as he mumbles ancient chants
and tosses his ravings into the air

drawing from violent seas
mariners' tales, from desert
sands caravans, from the Greek
our Helen's face and why not
when history is in his fist

But I the fool of fools
speaking in tongues and
feigning jokes, pleading
with him into day
until he sleeps like a baby

These visions fade
as I fall upon my pillow
There is a spot where
his head once lay but I
have wasted it, dreaming

Blue Skies

Oriane blue
just this side
of obsidian

One song breaks through
then follows a chorus
of warbling

Apollo blue
the scalding white
of noontide

Winged angels
propagate madly
in the heat

Olympus blue
streaked with
cirrus

Old firs
swing wildly
in the firmament

Poseidon blue
a slow blanket
transports the stars

Venus awakens
and sings love songs
to Mars

Crow and Sparrow: A Winter's Tale

In the days of old, Crow said to Sparrow,
"I own the winter, you must move along;
for your body is but a frail arrow
whilst mine is stouter and darker and strong.

"Plus the ground is hard for a bit sparrow
to eek out odd worms for his daily bread;
whilst there is meat on the straight and narrow,
there is naught for the both of us," Crow said.

"I will disappear," the sparrow entoned,
"but not because I am small in the end;
I leave because Père Winter has disowned
the crisp green seeds upon which I depend.

"You need not suffer so sadly, Frère Crow,
out of concern for a little sparrow."

before the fall

if i learn one lesson
let it be this
there is a tripwire
in my consciousness
and in front of it is a pit
that is endless

once my foot gets caught
and i begin to fall
my eyes will be blinded
by sand and rock
and my ears shall erupt
in the rapid tumbling

my mouth will utter
bits of jumbled tongue
and i won't know what
i am saying anymore
as the centuries rush past
ringed with corpses

and all because another
injured my pride
and all because my ego
was brushed and bruised
and who am i and who are you
on this battlefield

if i am to remain true
let me finish in beauty
my life on this planet

and let me never forget
that we were one person
before we were two

Millennium Song

Eve of the millennium
and what do I feel?
Despair and tribulation
Deep sadness and fear

A night of introspection
not a thread of what's real
as the TV drones on
with reports of world cheer

Each countdown a letdown
Each hour more pain
as I lay on the couch
coffee cup in my hand

Singing my own song
a silent refrain:
"It takes more than a millennium
to make a grain of sand"

Walking With Crows

Words words
what good are they
when every day
just hurts too much
and there's nothing
left but the
rush of the drug
and crows that
descend outside
my window

Pecking at the
leftover crumbs
on the side of the road
leftover songs
that flood my soul
in spite of
the hopelessness
the black hopelessness
of crows

Outside my door
they gather
those tremendous
black-winged wonders
witless survivors
of a winter sky
and a driving rain
until there is nothing
left to peck at when
the roads wash away

Yet still we
go walking
the crows weaving
in and out of the
trees above me
making circles
in this lonely
endless hungry
place of pain and
it doesn't matter that
we're going nowhere

What matters is
the moment of
power and glory
in the morning
when a certain drug
combination saves
my pain-filled body
fires the leaden
and brings it back
again to being

And to crows
and yet more crows
and a crow song
in my head
like a death threat
but blessed
because we're
still alive
and we're going somewhere

Catalog of a Rainy Day in December

i awake in a mound of cotton
quilt and brain tied in
in a fabric knot
my mouth dry and acerbic
and the sound of raindrops
beating the tile roof
droplets converging into
one sound, one contiguous thought
i am leaving soon
there is no turning back

the mountains are still standing
but leaves that once covered
branches are now gone
rainwater washes down gutters
and puddles under arches
and dampens my dry eyes as
i sit up to think
but thinking is not an option
when the day is fraught with water
and i with no tears to greet it

the once eternally blue sky
is gray-white and startling
i sit in the cotton void and
listen, surprised by birdsong
and the catalog of nonthought
that forms a large ellipse
in the center of this bed
and i at its edge, as so often
a figment of my own nonthought

disfigured like my blurry photographs

there is no hearth in which to
light a fire and burn away
the aftersense of ruinous dreams
there is no chimney to catch
the rising cottonous smoke of cigarettes
that carries me across boundaries
there is no stove on which
to make espresso, heat the
cereals of human evolution or
warm the soup of the soul

but there is water to
plump the flaking skin
water to fill the crevices
of failure, water flowing
water breaking, water without
rhyme or reason, and if i
had to chose but one element
for nourishment it would be water
because water is memory
its fluid body rippling in time

what i had then i have now
i need not think about it
let the cotton coverlet
fold again over eyes and lips
let me sleep in this soundfield
fade into nothingness or
into the ridicule of dreams
let this day stand in infamy
when rains flooded the earth
and drowned the foes of god

it is naught for nothing
that melancholy comes
with raindrops

Recovery Rag

I could languish over
Thermopylaes
then throw myself
into the sea
but I won't do it
I'm so glad I
washed the dishes
and my teeth last night
before I hit the bed
Bad habits sneak in
so easily
the self-pity
the paralysis
the disgust
like a lifelong practice
of apathy and self-abuse
Now I try
not to give up
put one foot forward
then trudge
make a phone call
finish the novel
open up the window
greet the day
then remind myself
one more time
that I'm worth it

Moineau's September Song

snowy cheer
hot toddies
white white hope
with bells pealing
an exchange of gifts
with St Nicholas
it's all cheap tyranny—

green buds
so what
then orange blossoms
a maypole
for the peasant
girls and boys
let them have it—

beauty queens on
red beaches
burning in the sun
jellyfish mob the shoreline
just give me an espresso
a big shady oak
and leave me alone—

but in September
en septembre
ton Septembrio
when I have to dig deep
under the cover of
new darkness
under the changing colors

when everything
is dying
when everything
has given up and
given in
to rain and worms
and the end of poems

when the mistral
whips through Provence
and drives the locals
mad with sound
when olives ripen and rot
and birds scatter
in great wave patterns

there you will find me
unearthing my heart
resurrecting my great body
and then flying
starting over
one more time
ad infinitum

Rondeau

Turn our gaze to the earth-filled grave
Far from kitchen and hovel cave
Where comely sons and daughters rest
In suits of ash, their lacy best
That mothers press and cannot save

We will not weep the more to crave
One last look at babes fair and brave
Little chicks in their yellowed nest
Brief brief the day

Turn our eyes to the sea's bright wave
That bears their souls from this enclave
Another hour our hearts to test
Brief brief the day

Winter Song

A winter song is springing
to my alerted ears,
the soft roar of rain
that replenishes my tears,
soaks open my heart,
and takes in the winter songs
of dead and dying poets.
I wash and dress their bodies,
gather the last autumn roses,
then lay them on a boat
for the long journey home.
Standing on the shore as rain
falls down upon my head,
I hope someone will care for me
as I have cared for them.

At the Stuck exhibit

Sin like a mirror
half-smiles at me as I cry
and if that's not enough
Lucifer is there to remind me
how lonely it gets
when your only light
is a pale crescent
Am I Apollo or Dionysus?
I can't tell anymore
damned if I do and
damned if I don't on this
big dark canvas of
forever twilight
Like Sisyphus it's the
same hills same valleys
and if that's not enough
the sky is on fire
and I find the symbolist anchors
of my childhood
I lie like Judith
I seduce and I kill
and what I get is more revenge
than you can shake a stick at
my own reflection cast
back to me as Sin
and Pietà, Pietà will always be mine
Pity my sons do not love me

little worlds

my little world of pain and beauty
accurate words for a poem
yet false notes in a throat
in two languages or in tongues
unspoken, choked, or broken

little world of the beloved
who pleases, who makes music
for the fat lazy queen
half dead on her flower bed
drowning in honeyed tea

lost sons and lovers
who descend or do not descend
with or without kisses
i do not attend: i am sending
love signals on transparent wings

this little world of energy
thought, neuron, heart
experienced through the
velvet glove of lust and fear
the end flashing like neon

this world far away where
a woman bathes her children
with tears, feeds them rock soup
buries them in sackcloth
while pulling out her hair

this burning world alive

where bully rockets smoke out
terrorists, miss their targets
propagate gangling workers
and sex up invading empires

and as the world bleeds
we cleanse and cauterize it
with a media whose tongues
mix pig slop with caviar
and call it plat du jour

worlds in worlds out
unfurling flags and anthems
bee songs all, all a day and
no more, each with vapid strophes
and wings so fast, they are invisible

i in this little world
a deathbed with hope strings
storyboards and heavy quilts
i sweat from head to foot
i sleep, dream, weep and wail

one world away from disaster
one away from orgasm and creation
i might need a god if not for poems
my dreamy eyes half closed
my ears plugged with seamless notes

battle scars

pile up the parched bones
roll them in parchment
make glue from the cartilage
bond hieroglyphs to soul

when you wake up
i shall take radiographs
bright spots on the nebula
men become idiots

love yourself love a soldier
when i hear the modern slogan
my mental projector starts up
i feel rashes and mosquito bites

in the x-ray of each fresh recruit
will burn the neuronic images
i carry a pack on my back as if i own it
i've got eyes for cameras

high alert!

we're in meltdown again
overhot, anxious, rapid heartbeat
blood is pooling at our ankles
away from the central nervous system
and lights are blinking
high alert! high alert! high alert!

with all these years under our belt
why didn't we tear down the intruder
why did we wait until he was here again
offering us his apocalyptic visions
spiraling us down to melting metals
poison gases and overproductive think tanks

high alert! i feel it in my belly
cover my breasts with my hands
buy iodine drops and call my parents
or try not to think about it at all
go about my daily life like a caged mouse
my throat raw and swollen

if we get through this one
will we change the energy trajectory
go for the sun moon and stars
or will we go on as before
separating molecules, merging gases
creating new cell lines, spawning new viruses

science is not coming to save us
it is creating monsters
and perhaps not one of them

but many intruders shall come calling
entering our lives and homes
stealing away our children

you shall feel

the bumpkin fell on her head last night
you could say she was inspired
she took a rocket from her purse
and lit the thing on fire

and all ablaze in a nuclear haze
she stumbled to the water
with one step on and one step off
her molecules got lighter

"i could not rest," she said to me
indicted by saintly crime
"when all around me is a hurt
i can no more imbibe

"i carried this old rocket 'round
through war and rape and riot
and when at last i needed it
i set the thing on fire"

the nuclear heat was wearing her down
her skin began to peel
but on that day i knew that she
at last began to feel

adieu pale beauty in a cloud
i shall miss having you around
but i understand your burning need
to launch yourself and let it bleed

remember us on earth below

if consciousness holds fast and true
but if it does not at least you are free
from this empathic poverty

vieillir

je voudrais m'étendre sur un vaste espace
puis me reculer dans ce grain de sable
la chanson du mistral est emplie de sel
le ciel gris ne peut retenir ses larmes

j'ai toutes les larmes en moi
j'ai un kyste qui s'enflamme sur le pubis
pour me faire reconnaitre ce que je suis
corps, sang, sueur

je ne vais pas m'élever cette fois
je suis atterrée pour de bon
l'aile cassée, je ne peux que regarder
les hirondelles s'envoler

je voudrais me pousser au bout
pour recommencer à zéro
mais on me trouvera à l'aube
vieille et sans bonté

l'aube

baisse les yeux
baisse-les
toi devant le miroir
de l'inconscient

sens les arbres
qui brûlent
dans la forêt
du temps

plus les années
avancent sur toi
plus une vague
avale ton nom

sache que
rien ne va rester
ni le sable doré
ni la terre dessous

ne pleure pas
de ta fin
pourquoi pleurer
devant l'inévitable

mieux dissiper
le sentiment d'unique
tout doit mourir
devant son miroir

ghosts

i live in the silence that
you have left behind
a deep abiding silence
that sweeps upon the room
when i hear a certain song
or come upon a photo
or just hear your names
bubbling up from the nowhere
that subtly subsume my thoughts
color them with blues and grays
as i struggle with chaos

a hole opens up in my chest
like some sacred chakra
reserved for your absence
and like an accident victim
i absorb the shock and turn
pale and parched with no
sense of myself
there is only you
moving in and out of my
peripheral vision
deepening a wound

all your ghosts inhabit this
house like crowds of
pilgrims, brides and children
you knock at my heart
in the wee morning hours
when i lie still and soundless
it is then that your subtle

bodies enter my mouth and
infiltrate my dreams
i grab for the coverlets
sad and shivering
I grab for goblets and drink up

there is no healing
there is only you encompassing
year after lonely year
there is only you in the music
there is you here in the snow and rain
or in the rays of sunshine
when i eat my soup
when i put on my clothes
i feel you watch me and
bid me come away
such the angel in me would love
but it is the animal that lives on

What Comes This Way

What comes this way
is not given without pain
It is not given without
sweat or a good
swat on the head

What comes this way
bends until vertigo sets in
with night fevers and dreams
that awaken you in screams
and tremors and self-blames

What comes this way
costs more than your right arm
or all you could pinch
in a lifetime of flinching
or the jewel passed down

from your great-grandmaman's dowry
or handwoven silk wound
round the world ten times
or the sunken wreck of
a pirate's laden ship

What comes this way
is always hungry and
tugs at your belly and
growls its demands until
you just can't stand it

What comes this way
is more illness than the
black plague visited upon us
every child, woman and man
carried away her slave

What comes this way
is never a bandage but rather
an opener for all your wounds
until you've bled to death and
stand white as the sands

What comes this way
even if you haven't asked
even if you hide yourself
in a deep mountain chasm
she will find you still

and you will have to ask then
you'll be made to demand
forgiveness for every major
or minor or unconscious sin
you have laden her with

For what comes this way
is brief and hard and
so full of longing that
even kings fall to the floor
in her terrible presence

She knows your heart
She knows every song your
tongue has sung and every
wish you've listed and

she's waiting to give you

that one last fell blow
to break your ego and claim
your soul as her own
to remake you, reshape you
into almighty God

For what comes this way
may not be to your pleasing
but for the power of the
chord, you must be
reborn a flaming word

What It Took

What it took
was a flag at half-mast
What it took
was a houseful of clues
What it took
was the courage to listen
What it took
was a bottomless blues

The door to my attic
has come unlatched
Its trunks are filled
with outgrown clothes
The glass figurine
smashes to the floor
Its fragments glisten
like precious jewels

All that I am
I have been
And what I've seen
made movies
I watch the parting shots
and give credit
where credit is due:
Some to me, some to you

I celebrate my life again
remember friends and innocents
and wash the demons
from my eyes

and raise the flag
to its full height
and fly, my dear ones
overhead

FRENCH TRANSLATIONS

Dans le jardin
page 17

In the garden

Always these keys of antiquity
The tears come
one cannot stop them
The proud queens
smiling in their alabaster masks
their dresses long, their hair tied tight
But their daughters are nude
hunted, carried away, raped
by the gods and the sons of gods
in forms of animals

vieillir
page 113

growing old

i would like to extend into vast space
then recoil into this grain of sand
the song of the mistral is full of salt
the gray sky cannot retain its tears

i have all the tears in me
i have a cyst inflamed on my pubis
to remind me what i am
body, blood, sweat

i am not going to rise this time
i am grounded for good
broken wing, i can only watch
as the swallows fly off

i would like to push myself to the end
to begin again at zero
but you will find me at dawn
old and without goodness

l'aube
page 114

dawn

lower your eyes
lower them
you before the mirror
of the unconscious

feel the trees
that burn
in the forest
of time

more the years
advance on you
more a wave
swallows your name

know that
nothing will remain
neither the golden sands
nor the earth below them

do not cry
for your end
why cry
before the inevitable

better to dissipate
the feeling of unique
everything must die
before its mirror

ACKNOWLEDGMENTS

I would like to thank several people for making this book possible.

My publisher Glen Perice who believed in my poetry and made it happen. I cherish his friendship.

The artist Jeanie Tomanek of Grayhouse Studios in Atlanta, Georgia, who offered the cover image "Kore Falling" in support of small presses.

My friend Anne de Kermarec who accompanied the French poems in this book.

My family and my friends around the world who believed in me and helped me.

Thank you.

About the Author

Laura Tattoo was born in New York City and lived for extended periods in India, France, and Greece. While pregnant with her first child she traveled across Canada with a carnival and made cotton candy. She also picked pears for a large farm in Hood River, Oregon. A graduate of Portland State University in English and French, she won the Nina Mae Kellogg Award for writing and literary scholarship. For many years she worked in public broadcasting and wrote and produced educational videos. Laura translated the twelve albums of the late French rocker Alain Bashung and created the blog *Bashung in English*. Her blog *Moineau en France* has been visited over 200,000 times. She lives in Portland, Oregon.